SLEEPING
PREACHER

1991
Agnes Lynch Starrett
Poetry Prize

SLEEPING PREACHER

Julia Kasdorf

University of Pittsburgh Press

Pittsburgh • London

The publication of this book is supported by grants from the National Endowment for the Arts in Washington, D.C., a Federal agency, and the Pennsylvania Council on the Arts.

Published by the University of Pittsburgh Press, Pittsburgh, Pa. 15260
Copyright © 1992, Julia Kasdorf
All rights reserved
Manufactured in the United States of America
Printed on acid-free paper
Second printing, 1993

Library of Congress Cataloging-in-Publication Data

Kasdorf, Julia, 1962–
   Sleeping preacher / Julia Kasdorf.
      p.   cm.—(Pitt poetry series)
      ISBN 0-8229-3720-4 (cl : acid-free paper).—ISBN 0-8229-5480-X
(pb. : acid-free paper)
      I. Title. II. Series.
      PS3561.A6958S57   1991
      811'.54—dc20   92-50199
                                                          CIP

A CIP catalogue record for this book is available from the British Library.
Eurospan, London

The author and publisher wish to express their grateful acknowledgment to the following publications in which some of these poems first appeared: *Cincinnati Poetry Review* ("Cousins"); *Home Planet News* ("Piano, New York"); *The Journal* ("Green Market, New York"); *The Spoon River Quarterly* ("First TV in a Mennonite Family," "Uncle," "When Our Women Go Crazy"); *West Branch* ("Along Ocean Parkway in Brooklyn," "August," "Dying with Amish Uncles," "Handling Tools," "How to Think of Danger," "Mennonites," "Riding Bike with No Hands," "The Only Photograph of My Father as a Boy," "What I Learned from My Mother"); *Western Journal of Medicine* ("Older Brother"); and *Yarrow* ("Grossdaadi's Sale," formerly "Grossdaddy's Sale," "The View").

"I Carry Dead Vesta" was first published in *Festival Quarterly*, Fall, 1989. "Green Market, New York," was reprinted in this issue.

"Riding Bike with No Hands" was reprinted in the *Anthology of Magazine Verse & Yearbook of American Poetry, 1986–1988* (Monitor, 1988).

"Where We Are" was first published in *Looking for Home: Women Writing About Exile* (Milkweed Editions, 1990). "Green Market, New York," and "Mennonites," were reprinted in this volume.

Thanks to Donald Antrim, Suzanne Axtell, and Julia Lisella. I also appreciate the support of the MacDowell Colony, The Corporation of Yaddo, and the Ragdale Foundation. And most gratitude to David.

In memory of Bertha Peachey Spicher Sharpe, 1910–1990

Contents

SLEEPING
PREACHER

Green Market, New York

The first day of false spring, I hit the street,
buoyant, my coat open. I could keep walking
and leave that job without cleaning my desk.
At Union Square the country people slouch
by crates of last fall's potatoes.
An Amish lady tends her table of pies.
I ask where her farm is. "Upstate," she says,
"but we moved from P.A. where the land is better,
and the growing season's longer by a month."
I ask where in P.A. "Towns you wouldn't know,
around Mifflinburg, around Belleville."
And I tell her I was born there.
"Now who would your grandparents be?"
"Thomas and Vesta Peachey."
"Well, I was a Peachey," she says,
and she grins like she sees the whole farm
on my face. "What a place your folks had,
down Locust Grove. Do you know my father,
the harness shop on the Front Mountain Road?"
I do. And then we can't think what to say,
that Valley so far from the traffic on Broadway.
I choose a pie while she eyes my short hair
then looks square on my face. She knows
I know better than to pay six dollars for this.
"Do you live in the city?" she asks. "Do you like it?"
I say no. And that was no lie, Emma Peachey.
I don't like New York, but sometimes these streets
hold me as hard as we're held by rich earth.
I have not forgotten that Bible verse:
Whoever puts his hand to the plow and looks back
is not fit for the kingdom of God.

I Carry Dead Vesta

Vesta Peachey (1918–1962)

Vesta's daughter, my mother, home to mourn
with her father, carried me ripening,
swelling out like an embarrassment in that house
of death and drawn drapes.

To that house I was born, wailing and red,
the girl Vesta wanted when she papered
the parlor with blooming magnolias
and cardinals huge as old crows.

When old church ladies call me her name,
I must tell them I'm no one they know,
no one who stayed in that Valley of silos
and holsteins.

I have only her hair which, this short,
must look like it's up in a bun
and her wide mouth that opens too quickly
to eat or to speak.

I've only ever seen her in that photograph,
holding my older brother by a clump of white lilies
behind the farmhouse in Pennsylvania,
and she never held me.

But I have carried her out of that Valley,
between Front Mountain and Back;
I've taken her still clutching
her bulbs and berry canes.

Vesta's Father

Mom's in the kitchen telling stories
from before she was born, how Vesta figured
if her father quit smoking, he'd save enough
to buy new winter coats that she and her sisters
would not be ashamed to hang in the anteroom
of Locust Grove Mennonite Church,
where the ladies couldn't help but smell smoke
when the girls pressed around the mirror
to jab pins in their buns and straighten prayer coverings.
He drank, too. Deer season each year
when he went with the Hoot Owls to their camp
on Back Mountain, someone always brought him home, drunk,
to his wife, who had spells when she couldn't stop crying.
The bishop found out he wore a baseball cap
and made him confess that worldliness
to the whole congregation. And when he died,
with whiskey on his nightstand,
he was buried by the Lutherans.

Tears gleam on Mother's cheeks
as she traces the grain in the table boards,
but I am not weeping like his wife or daughters.
The sins of the fathers won't be visited
on my generation. I say there is no shame
in lying among Lutherans where folks are allowed
to put flowers on graves, his plot in plain view
of those mountains that rise dark and silent
as old Mennonites standing in pews—
black-stockinged women on one side,
black-suited men on the other—
those mountains so high they slow the sunrise
and hurry the night.

The Sleeping Preacher

About the time guilt got the best
of the Fox sisters, and they confessed
the rappings were not messages
from the dead to comfort their friends,
but only the girls' toe knuckles cracking,
about that time, the Sleeping Preacher came
to the Valley. Our great-grandma saw him
swoon across the front pew
and preach against jewelry,
fancy dresses for women, and photographs.
That day she threw all the old daguerreotypes
in gilt and red velvet cases, all the prints
of her parents on their wedding day,
of the milk wagon parked outside their barn,
and herself in high button shoes
into the cookstove. She stoked those flames
to burn away the sins
that might keep her kin from rising
on the last day. She did not think of us,
only to save us, leaving nothing
for us to touch or see
except this stubborn will to believe.

When Our Women Go Crazy

When our women go crazy, they're scared there won't be
enough meat in the house. They keep asking
but how will we eat? Who will cook? Will there be enough?
Mother to daughter, it's always the same
questions. The sisters and aunts recognize symptoms:
      she thinks there's no food, same as Mommy
      before they sent her away to that place,
      and she thinks if she goes, the men will eat
      whatever they find right out of the saucepans.
When our women are sane, they can tomatoes
and simmer big pots of soup for the freezer.
They are satisfied arranging spice tins
on cupboard shelves lined with clean paper.
They save all the leftovers under tight lids
and only throw them away when they're rotten.
Their refrigerators are always immaculate and full,
which is also the case when our women are crazy.

St. Francis Preaches to the Birds

In a thirteenth-century fresco,
St. Francis preaches to blackbirds
lined up on boughs that grow
unnaturally straight. "Like old crows
on a telephone line," Mom recalled
that row of Mennonite girls up front
for baptism: dark stockings on
thin legs, long black sleeves
(because elbows, like knees, suggest),
and the extra flap in front
to hide breasts just beginning
to swell behind nips. Preach to
those birds, St. Francis,
convert them from crows
into the doves wise Solomon loved,
let the ones that would suckle me
lift that cloth and flap off
into the morning sun, wings
above a gaping congregation.

A Family History

At dusk the girl who will become my mom
must trudge through the snow, her legs
cold under skirts, a bandanna tight on her braids.
In the henhouse, a klook pecks her chapped hand
as she pulls a warm egg from under its breast.
This girl will always hate hens,
and she already knows she won't marry a farmer.
In a dim barn, my father, a boy, forks hay
under the holsteins' steaming noses.
They sway on their hooves and swat dangerous tails,
but he is thinking of snow, how it blows
across the gray pond scribbled with skate tracks,
of the small blaze on its shore, and the boys
in black coats who skate hand-in-hand
round and round, building up speed
until the leader cracks that whip
of mittens and arms, and it jerks around
fast, flinging off the last boy.
He'd be that one—flung like a spark
trailing only his scarf.

The Mean Words of Jesus

In the home movies that run endlessly
through my head, Grandpa offers Dad
a new car if he'll quit school at sixteen
to help run the farm. And Dad turns him down.
Then the other Grandpa offers Mom
a store-bought dress if she'll stay home
from college to take care of her mother.
She doesn't want a dress that much,
but stays, and one of his cows fetches enough
to pay tuition at a nursing school nearby.
When her mother finally dies, Mom's home again
for six months, cooking and cleaning, giving
birth to me while my father works miles away.
This is the part I cannot stand to see
another time. Here I edit the scenes
and reverse all their consequences. Here
my mother must turn to her father
at the last moment, when the music swells
unbearably as in the last scene of *Casablanca,*
and in that soft, trembling light,
the mean words of Jesus must fly
from her lips: Who is my mother?
or better yet: Let the dead bury the dead.
Here she must announce, "I can't reproduce
her cream sauce or spotless windows;
let the strawberries rot on the vine
if no one will pick them." Here she'll remember
her mother's high school diploma, framed
and stern as a clock above the cookstove,
earned while younger sisters dropped out
to work in a bakery, take in laundry,
scrub rich people's floors, and their mother
grew sicker in body and soul.

The Only Photograph of My Father as a Boy

In Amish trousers and suspenders,
he's barefoot by the field lane,
blond hair bowl-cut, his face twisted.
He knows this shouldn't be—
this worldly uncle squinting into a box
camera, commanding, "Hold still."
That click, something flew out of him
with, "Don't tell your mother 'bout this."
And something flew in. The next picture,
high school graduation, he's grinning
on the rim of the world,
as confident as science in 1951.

Song of Enough

The first frosts, my father, still without shoes,
chased in the cows for milking, leaping
from spot to tropical spot where they'd lain.
On Christmas mornings he'd find only socks
on his plate, and a sprinkling of hay
where the reindeer had been. In summer his mother
used black-market sugar to can—
the greater sin, to leave the peaches to rot.
When damp bales of hay burst into flame,
he ran from the barn to kneel by her bed,
her blond hair splayed on the pillow case,
her fevered face bright as an angel's.
The parlor was never as silent as when
black-clothed relatives came to sit
for the loss of the barn, before all the men
came back in their work clothes
to hammer timbers into trusses and hoist
cross beams against that clear sky.
Nor as silent as when they returned
to sit with his mother's body, on chairs
drug in from the kitchen, while he sobbed
alone behind the new barn. When he came home
from college, dreaming at last in English,
he reached for words that didn't exist
in Pennsylvania Dutch to talk with his aunts,
and for the first time wondered what you could think
if all you spoke was a language with words enough
for cooking and farm work and gossip.

Grossdaadi's Funeral

This is the child in a buff-colored coat with a foxtail collar.
This is the child who walks down the aisle between straight-back
    benches
in Amish church; gapes at great-aunts and great-uncles and covens
of cousins in black.

This is the child whose momma knows she'll see plenty of this
and lifts her to the bare, pine box that Grossdaadi made for
    himself.
(He crawled in to test, then kept it locked in a spare bedroom
back at the farm.)

This is the child who stares at his hand, bony and veined,
covered with skin like the paper her momma wraps sandwiches in;
she touches his face chilled by the aunts who sat up all night
sponging the corpse.

This is the child who fingers his beard, as gray as the fur
on the foxhead muff that dangles from grosgrain around her neck.
Later she'll learn the hair of the dead—like this dirty gauze beard—
still grows in the grave.

This is the girl who clutches the muff, who digs in its fur
for edges of skull, scrapes at the glass beads glued in for eyes,
and presses the teeth so her fingertips sting
all through the long, German prayers.

Grossdaadi's Sale

While Amish uncles nod their bids
for German Bibles, work gloves, canning jars,
we sneak upstairs to press our tongues
against the frozen windowpanes.
We kneel on the grate in the floor
to warm our cheeks and peer on parlor ferns,
crocheted flakes draped on dark sofas,
and the foil plaque that warns, "Do nothing
you would not like to be doing when Jesus comes."

Below, Ernest, the idiot son of cousins
who married too close, picks his nose
by the oil stove. We hiss his name
until he balks and grunts and swings
with a rage that would smash the panes
of the corner cupboard, splinter cup handles
as easily as he hoists bales of hay.
We jump to the bed and squeal
in the quilts, gripped by the secret
we'll share until we grow
too embarrassed to remember
this or that barn cat
we dropped from the hayloft.

Dying with Amish Uncles

The ground was frozen so hard
his sons used a jackhammer to pry
open a grave in the rocky field
where Grossdaadi's wife and daughter
lay under the streaked stones
that tell only last names:
Yoder, Zook, Yoder.

Amish uncles, Grossdaadi's sons,
shoveled earth on the box;
stones clattered on wood then quieted
while we sang hymns to the wind.
Bending over the hole,
Uncle Kore wouldn't wipe
his dripping nose and chin.

Ten years later when we gather
for July ham and moon pies,
the uncles stand to sing
Grossdaadi's favorite hymns.
At *"Gott ist die Liebe,"*
they almost laugh
with the tears running
into their beards;
Abe and Mose and Ben
do not wipe them.

Their voices come deep as graves
and unashamed of shirtsleeves
or suspenders. Seeing them cry
that brave, I think the uncles
mustn't die, that they'll stay
with those of us who must,
being so much better than we are
at weathering death.

Leftover Blessings

His dinner on the stove, Grandpa smirked at our jar
of pickled eggs and beets, "Old maids' picnic,
party for hens." They still let Bertha come
since she married so late and someone so mean.
(Who could begrudge all those children a mother,
besides it was she who taught that proud Amishman
to drive in her own new, black Plymouth.)

They had a spot under the hemlocks
by a stream on Back Mountain, the Valley's
leftover blessings: Elsie and Miriam,
the three Stayrook sisters who crocheted and sang,
and Mary and Loamie who lived on the home farm
like girls—calling all the chickens by name,
milking goats and Rosie the cow by hand,
feeding geese and guinea hens just for fun.
Winters they hooked rugs from wool rags,
heating only one room in that great, dark house.

The only child among women, I couldn't imagine
them young or waiting for dates, though I'd seen
the photograph from Rehoboth or one of the ocean cities—
five of them lined up, laughing in the surf,
thin, dark-haired, hiking their skirts.
I never guessed they might have chosen
to stay with women.

I only felt the weight of the way
they heaped my plate and touched my hair,
or the picnic games they made only for me.
How they cheered while I raced against
invisible children, sparing me the indignity
of three-legged relays, bestowing balloons
and butterscotch. So much for just one child,

I thought. This is what it means to be a blessing,
enough love left over to give prizes for nothing,
for just showing up, being young, being born
the granddaughter of a man someone married.

Where We Are

Bertha let me run barefoot those weeks
at her house. I learned Bible verses
and picked red-stem peppermint from cow creeks
for the tea she steeped in milk jugs.
Thor stem we hung to dry in the attic
for Grandpa's stomach. She called flies
the Mister and Misses we mustn't let in
through the breezeway where *Fleissig Lizzies*
bloomed in the windows. In the cellar
she peeled peaches while steam clattered the lid
of a speckled canner, and I scampered
behind her, "Three guesses, where am I?"
And she'd guess, "Under the steps? Behind
the jam closet? Back of the box of cans
Daddy should dump off the mountainside soon?"
But I'd be in the dark root cellar, crouched
with sprouting potatoes under shelves of jars
that reached to the ceiling: three kinds of pickles,
green and wax beans, red, white, and sour cherries,
and the horrible beef canned in its tallow.
Three guesses, where am I? Her letters still find me.
On paper printed with birds and Bible verses
she writes, "Greetings in Jesus' name.
Come for a weekend, a week. And we must thank God
you will not stay in that city forever."
Instead, I thank God I can still find her
poking her pots of African violets or bent
over the counter, crimping the crust on a pie.
She's still there in that silence, bowing her head
before meals, breathing desirous prayers
or remembering how she flew home to us,
Grandpa's corpse hidden deep in the plane,
how from takeoff to landing she stitched
garlands of daisies on quilt blocks,
her needle tacking black knots on the blooms,

so wherever I use this quilt,
I'll see those seeds and think of Grandpa.
Yet it's her I see, hunched in the soft spot
of airplane light, embroidering above him, alive.

August

Dad's mother was coming home
from picking huckleberries on the mountain
when sunlight spooked the horse, and it tore
through a pasture fence, dragging the buggy
until it broke lose, hurling the children,
killing their mother, spilling
those silver pails of sweet, black fruit.
Mom's mother, just forty-five and already a grandma,
was walking the hill to Locust Grove Church
when she clutched the bodice of her Sunday dress
and slumped to the berm, just past grandpa's silo
filled with the summer's rotting fodder.
And this stepmother, the only grandmother
I've loved, canned fourteen quarts of peaches
before gasping, stumbling, leaving us
with only her corpse and china closet.
Her sister, Elsie, hopes she looks this good for church,
but in such heat, she tells me, things turn.
Our backs and thighs sweat to the pews
during the sermon so full of that fiery lake
we can taste the sinners' thirst. From the grave,
families drift across the grass to older stones.
Strange, how it was a day like this in '48, they say,
in '62. It's true. August takes the mothers
in this family unexpectedly, while tomatoes burst
their skins, and sweet corn bulges with the smut
that blackens your fingers pulling back the husk.
And under this hot sun, what woman can resist—
how easy it becomes to just lie back
and let your womb swell, like all the rest.

Freindschaft

*Be ye not unequally yoked together with
unbelievers: for what fellowship hath
righteousness with unrighteousness? and what
communion hath light with darkness?*

—II Corinthians 6:14

At the Yoder reunion, there are always more children
than grown-ups. Outside the white, Amish school
they run barefoot, identical: girls with buns
under starched coverings, boys in blue shirts
and suspenders. In the basement, between long tables
of food, cousins and aunts trace family lines
that grow tangled and thick as root-bound plants:
two sisters who married two brothers
makes their twenty-some children twice cousins.

A ten-year-old girl, the length of a doll,
sighs like a miniature deaconess
in her cape dress and covering the size of a teacup.
Her sisters pass her down the bench
while a man with spidery eyebrows
and a clenched forehead circles around them,
pointing at pictures of tractors.
His thick tongue writhes on his lips
and refuses to speak.

~

My great-uncle Smiley Joe
told Uncle Tom,
when Tom proposed
to his third cousin,
who is also Joe's niece,
"Women are clover,
the closer to home you find them,
the sweeter they are."

21

~

As I grow up, the great-aunts click their tongues.
They are looking for signs of their lives
in my limbs: It's the Hartzler blood that makes you
dark and thin. It's just like Aunt Toot to love
olives and pickles and fuss like a hen.
Your Yoder nose. Those Spicher ways—
you know, your grandpa ran from house to barn
to get the milking done before his neighbors.
You can't help it, the Peachey in you
makes you faint at the sight of your blood.
You think you're the first, but your grandma
sewed a two-piece swimsuit and wore it
until the bishop found out. You can see
scraps of that wild yellow challis
sewn in her quilt.

They search my life for proof that I am the same
as the alcoholic great-grandpa
or his pious wife, who died insane,
the same as my sobbing mom,
who refused to get out of the car
at a family reunion, the same
as that shriveled great-uncle
who reeked of sweat and stared me to silence
with his bright, terrified eyes.

~

With parents who are distant cousins and their
parents cousins before, my greatest fears
get told in the stories I already know.
What can I do to change my fate
but take a strange lover and cleave
to my work? The Amish believe

it is sinful to be sure
their souls are saved.
The only defense against their worst fears
is work and hope, *arbeite und hoffe.*
The work that they mean
darkens your skin with sun
and roughens your hands; you must strain
as a horse against a harness, as light
against the darkness.

Along Ocean Parkway in Brooklyn

Three Hasidic boys talk like Amishmen,
hands in their long black coats that flap open
at the knees, heads nodding under hats.

They do not raise their pale, Prague cheeks
as I walk by. I am the world to them,
as I would have been to my father,

who once stood like this, speaking low German
in a knot of boys at the edge of an auction lot.
Which of these will be the one to leave

our neighborhood of lavish bakeries
closed up tight for Passover,
as though leavening might leak into the streets

and keep the Children of Israel in Egypt?
I bless the one who leaves in anger or hurt,
bless the memory of his first cheeseburger

and the mind that returns for the rest of his life
to this corner, to the Hebrew storefronts
where old men drink dark tea in tumblers.

I praise equally the ones who stay
clustered like Amish farms in the dusk,
no phone lines running in, no circle

of light in the farmyards—
house, barn, coop, and crib
on the edge of the fields.

That Story

In this story, the Garden of Eden is the Valley;
Adam and Eve are the parents who left
all those fine holsteins and the swallows
darting under the barn beams at dusk.
Once out of the Garden, they had to find jobs,
so Eve became a nurse, silent witness to the world's ills,
and Adam was doomed to office work. In the evenings
he pushed a plow in his garden's poor soil,
while his children stooped over the furrows
behind him, trailing pebbles of fertilizer
from their fists, dropping seeds
painted pesticide pink.

In this story, Cain is a woman
who slays with words. She moves to the city
where she fusses over a Christmas cactus
and African violets in pots. Her garden is only as wide
as a sidewalk; stray cats pee on her ragged
tomato stalks. Sometimes she thinks back to the nights
she and her father, tired together, sat
on the edge of their patch. Now she knows
his silent longing for that Garden.
It is easy to believe that story
and to grow as weary
as Israel's children
by the waters of Babylon.

First TV in a Mennonite Family

1968

The lid of the Chevy trunk couldn't close
on that wooden console with a jade screen
and gold flecks in the fabric over the speaker.

They sent us to bed then set it up
in the basement, as far from our rooms
and the dinner table as they could get,

out of sight for grandparents' visits.
The first morning, Mother studied the guide
and chose Captain Kangaroo for me,

but when we turned it on, the point of light
on the screen grew into black-and-white men
lifting a stretcher into the back of an ambulance.

Each click of the huge, plastic knob
flashed the same men, the same ambulance door
propped back like a broken wing.

After that, we were forbidden to watch everything
except the Captain and "I Love Lucy."
Yet, when Dad returned from business in Chicago,

I heard him tell Mom how police beat the kids
under his hotel window, and I knew whatever it was,
that vague, distant war had finally come.

Uncle

At nine I knew what Jesus would do
if he got C.O. just for being born
Mennonite. He'd go anyway, like you.

In the name of peace, he'd race
an ambulance through the screaming streets
of Saigon. He'd grow a moustache to show
he wasn't a soldier—a speck
on the camera lens, Grandpa insisted.

He'd take a generator to a village
in the hills where golden children
would run behind him yelling, "Mother Fucker."

He'd thrust brilliant green blades
of rice into the fields where men's legs
and the torsos of water buffaloes exploded
when plows struck bombs in the mud.

When the planes returned, he'd load
whomever he could into the only car,
drive to a refugee camp, and there give up
at last, as you gave up bearing that war
on your tall, blond body.

Lost across the continents for months,
you returned to us, the uncle of someone else,
gaunt as a corpse, pale and haunted.
And when you could barely finish
a child's portion at Howard Johnson's,
that was the only miracle I could grasp.

Grackles

The first spring I could read, I found pictures
in *Life* magazine of the Vietcong
who rammed chopsticks in children's ears
to keep them from hearing the wrong politics.
Playing under the jack pines behind the house,
my brother would scream, "Chopsticks!"
to see me shriek and clutch my ears.
But I listened when he explained, we kill
grackles—those beautiful blackbirds whose necks
shine purple—because they pull up seed corn
by its first leaves to eat the sprouting kernels.
And I stood by while he thrust the bent end
of a curtain rod into a nest under the eaves
of the tool shed, where the baby birds cheeped.

Cousins

Pennsylvania, 1987

We have nothing to say to each other,
my favorite cousin and I, though we share
the same shape of a nose, the same eyes.
In our silence, her son plants kernels of corn
in straight rows on the carpet between us.
His curls are fine as silk on green corn;
the perfect loaves of his arms are smoother
than dough. At two he already knows
manure spreader, front loader, tractor,
but he cannot tell me the colors
of his new John Deere or the red harrow disc
he drags behind it.

Like his mother and me, this boy will hide
lightning-bug jewels in a Band Aid box.
His hands will blacken with dandelion milk;
he will flick off their yellow heads and slit
their hollow stems so they coil like spit curls.
He will draw tadpoles from the watering trough,
clutch them until they grow sticky and still.
He'll catch a barn cat by the tail
then let it fly against the cement milk house.
It will stagger, drunk, by the wall, a red bead
trailing from its nose. Like us,
this boy will be raised to fear cities.

The Interesting Thing

The interesting thing is not that a boy
could cut off the head of a doll with a toy
saw. The interesting thing is that the parents
would blame the girl, because she had a new baby brother.
The interesting thing is not that the brother
would hang a plastic baby from a limb
and tie his sister to the trunk beneath it,
her ankles and wrists burned by rope, but that,
when found, she would insist,
"A neighbor did this." The thing is not
that an old neighbor would wave the girl in
on her way home from school to show her
seedlings sprouting under a violet Gro-Lux light
in his basement, not that he would wheeze
in her ear, or even that he would stab
his tobacco-sweet tongue against her teeth,
but that the girl would walk home,
spitting out the taste of him
and tell no one.

Older Brother

August afternoons when the sky darkened with storms,
we'd climb the old silver maple
high as its limbs could hold us
and ride that wind that rocked the wren house
and turned grape leaves to their white undersides
down on the arbor. He'd lean into it
like a prow, his hair cowlicked back,
seeming to stare at something beyond
our hills of sheep and junkyards, unflinching
even when rain spattered his glasses.

That's how I think he looks now,
walking on silent shoes through the wards,
delivering news to families too stunned to question
the voice that pronounces so surely
stillbirth or the names of cancers.
But I wonder if there is ever a father,
a mill worker with large, blackened fists
who grabs the narrow lapels of his lab coat
and pounds on my brother's chest,
demanding that he take it back.

Catholics

for Julia

In third grade all the girls got confirmed
and had their ears pierced. They flaunted
those dingy threads that hung from their lobes,
telling how the ice stung, how the cartilage crunched
when the needle broke through, how knots
in the thread had to be pulled through the holes,
one each day, like a prayer on the rosary.

At recess I turned the rope
while Michelle skipped and spun and counted to ten,
and a scapular leapt from the neck of her dress.
She dangled that pale pink ribbon,
a picture of the Blessed Mother on one end
and the Sacred Heart on the other,
saying, "This is my protection, front and back."
That was when I called them Catholic
and said, "Your people killed my people;
your priests threw a man into a river,
tied in a sack with a dog, a cat, a rooster, a snake,
think how they scratched and bit going down,
think how they drowned. Your priests
burned holes in the tongues of our preachers,
and put pacifists naked in cages
to starve and rot while the birds
pecked off their flesh."

Michelle and Vicki and Lisa just looked at me,
the jump rope slack as a snake
at our feet. But in my memory
I want these girls with fine bones and dark eyes
to speak up:

those priests were not me,
those martyrs weren't you,
and we have our martyr stories, too.
I want to take their slim girl-bodies into my arms
and tell them I said it only because
I wanted to wear a small, oval metal
I could pull from my T-shirt to kiss
before tests. I wanted a white communion dress,
and to pray with you
to your beautiful Blessed Mother in blue.

Mennonites

We keep our quilts in closets and do not dance.
We hoe thistles along fence rows for fear
we may not be perfect as our Heavenly Father.
We clean up his disasters. No one has to
call; we just show up in the wake of tornadoes
with hammers, after floods with buckets.
Like Jesus, the servant, we wash each other's feet
twice a year and eat the Lord's Supper,
afraid of sins hidden so deep in our organs
they could damn us unawares,
swallowing this bread, his body, this juice.
Growing up, we love the engravings in *Martyrs Mirror:*
men drowned like cats in burlap sacks,
the Catholic inquisitors,
the woman who handed a pear to her son,
her tongue screwed to the roof of her mouth
to keep her from singing hymns while she burned.
We love Catherine the Great and the rich tracts
she gave us in the Ukraine, bright green winter wheat,
the Cossacks who torched it, and Stalin,
who starved our cousins while wheat rotted
in granaries. We must love our enemies.
We must forgive as our sins are forgiven,
our great-uncle tells us, showing the chain
and ball in a cage whittled from one block of wood
while he was in prison for refusing to shoulder
a gun. He shows the clipping from 1916:
Mennonites are German milksops, too yellow to fight.
We love those Nazi soldiers who, like Moses,
led the last cattle cars rocking out of the Ukraine,
crammed with our parents—children then—
learning the names of Kansas, Saskatchewan, Paraguay.
This is why we cannot leave the beliefs
or what else would we be? why we eat

'til we're drunk on shoofly and moon pies and borscht.
We do not drink; we sing. Unaccompanied on Sundays,
those hymns in four parts, our voices lift with such force
that we lift, as chaff lifts toward God.

Clear Night at the End of the Twentieth Century

for Jerry

The light we call stars has traveled
a great distance to shine above this field
rimmed by black pines in New Hampshire.
Whatever we see in each other must be
the distance we've come in our lives
and all we've brought with us. Though we shared
the same dinner tonight, the food that sustained
our parents still sustains us:
>the pig slaughtered and smoked
>in a cold November farmyard,
>the tray of herrings in sour cream
>from a chilled case at the Appetizing.

Though we cling to the few words of Yiddish
that match Pennsylvania Dutch,
our mothers could never have spoken,
and that distance also exists between us.
It is as though we try to make love,
and our bed keeps filling with forebears
who bicker at such a furious pitch
we cannot tell the oppressors from victims.
Jews rode in cattle cars east to their deaths,
and the wives and children of Mennonites
rode west in those cars, bound for Berlin,
delivered from Stalin. Opa wore
a Hitler moustache and slicked his hair
in the thirties, reading German propaganda
in Canada, refusing to speak
one more word of Russian. Old and blind,
he still detests red, even in sunsets.

You said if you saw someone drowning,
the only kind of person you might not save
would be German, but you probably would
throw a rope even to one of us.

The Body Remembers

for David

Before they were married, Opa slept
on the floor beside Oma's bed.
The wedding feast was just
cabbage soup, not a bone
to cook in the village.
Even in Canada, Oma stewed borscht
without beef. In California, among orchards,
your mother cooks *geschmuade Bonen*
without ham. The body remembers
famine, but I make *Kartoffelsuppe*
thick with cream and stroke
your white ribs with my lips.
I kiss your stomach, innocent as a fish,
and crush my small, olive breasts
on your chest. The blades
of our pelvises collide
in defiance of grief
as we pull and thrust
against all the suffering
sown in our cells, all those stories
of bodies enduring torture and hunger
for God. We knock together
like two muddy shoes, knocking
history loose from our limbs,
knocking through Zurich and Danzig,
knocking off kulak and milksop
(all the names they once called us),
knocking until we are nothing special,
just a woman and man on a floor
in Brooklyn, where Arab melodies
and Burmese cooking waft
through our windows like ghosts.

What Language Is For

—Genesis 11:4

The blond son, the blue-eyed boy, brings me home.
I am dark and don't speak German. On the phone
in *Plautdietsch*, his mother tells Aunt Margaret,
"A beauty she's not, but she has beautiful eyes."

Knitting needles click perfect stitches
as she tells me: Glastnost—this we have seen
before, and famine and revolution,
one fortune sunk in the Channel, one
sunk in Siberian dirt, as if we'd return.

And the ones sent back from Moscow or Berlin,
nothing to go home to but mines.
Some are still there, and at night
men gather to sing softly
the hymns in German.

She tells how Hans, born in Siberia but
raised on manioc and fish caught in baskets,
could court her in Canada—
English and Portuguese, yes, but
Plautdietsch is the language of love
and housework.

When I love her son or pray
for him, it is always in English.
The dialects have slipped from our tongues
except where words stick to the foods
and feelings English can't name:
Schlopst du?
Mein Liebchen, schlopst du?

How to Think of Danger

for David

While you're in the kitchen doing dishes,
I'm in bed on the edge of sleep, listening
to the clink of plates and silverware, the surge
of rinse water. Was it ever this good
for my mother? Did she and Dad collapse
laughing under their bright ring of kitchen light?
Did they forget to lock doors or pull blinds?
Did the Angel of Death glide down their street
but stop only to slay the children and pets
of strangers?

Before I was born, did Mom think of danger
when the Angel's breath touched her,
and gas flames leapt from the burner to melt
her negligee and char the tender hollow
under her arm? Did Dad finally know danger
alone, returned to their dark apartment
stinking of smoke and burnt flesh, carpets
heaped where she rolled to smother flames?

We don't know how to think of danger
in this house we rent without insurance
or money in the bank. We're adolescents
who can out-drive accidents.
Yet while we sleep, out in our kitchen
the pilot lights deep in the old stove
glow blue phosphorescence in the burner wells,
four beacons that never go out.

Their Marriage

The bridesmaids' breasts, swathed in aqua
and yellow satin to match the table's bunting,
suddenly look ridiculous. Everyone's stunned,
especially my mother, her dark eyes
a confusion of pleasure and hurt.
From her place at the center of the table
before a fire hall of 400, she saw it all—
her Uncle Manny who'd married them
a few hours before, Aunt Elsie's stiff face,
the ambulance men, the stretcher whisked out
between tables of guests, "Stand back,
give him air." But he was already dead.
Who could eat? Who could even *be* at a reception
at a time like this? Might as well save the cake
for the funeral lunch.

What did the poor things think—an omen, a symbol—
then, or later that night on Back Mountain
in a borrowed cottage smelling of mildew and wood smoke
where they struggled to teach one another a sex
no longer forbidden. Just twenty-four and twenty-one,
smooth-skinned, hopelessly beautiful in their passion,
too young to guess what lay before them, behind them.
Still smarting in his arms, while the night swelled
with birdsong and dawn tinted the tiny room,
could she guess even then that marriage
is mostly an awkward three-legged walk?

Blood

David pulls his cut hand from the dishpan,
limp fish dripping blood and soap suds.
What do I do? What would my mother do?
Grab a tea towel and ice, and say, "Press it,"
then, "You must get stitches." He refuses
like Dad, who returned the chain saw
before getting his toe sewn, his sneaker
leaking blood on the accelerator.
I grab money, run twenty blocks to the drug store
panting, "Blood, blood is what comes
out of us." Before, he looked so fine,
eating spaghetti, his blood inside.
Strange how we forget,
how well we hide whatever is in us,
how Mother once cut white butterflies
to tape my brother's head shut.

What I Learned from My Mother

I learned from my mother how to love
the living, to have plenty of vases on hand
in case you have to rush to the hospital
with peonies cut from the lawn, black ants
still stuck to the buds. I learned to save jars
large enough to hold fruit salad for a whole
grieving household, to cube home-canned pears
and peaches, to slice through maroon grape skins
and flick out the sexual seeds with a knife point.
I learned to attend viewings even if I didn't know
the deceased, to press the moist hands
of the living, to look in their eyes and offer
sympathy, as though I understood loss even then.
I learned that whatever we say means nothing,
what anyone will remember is that we came.
I learned to believe I had the power to ease
awful pains materially like an angel.
Like a doctor, I learned to create
from another's suffering my own usefulness, and once
you know how to do this, you can never refuse.
To every house you enter, you must offer
healing: a chocolate cake you baked yourself,
the blessing of your voice, your chaste touch.

After the Second Miscarriage

for Ellen

There are no guarantees in marrying doctors
or men who'd make suitable fathers.
I tell you, it has nothing to do with us
whether babies stay or slink out,
bloody lumps in the toilet, in the swirl
of the flush. Remember that summer,
the night we dropped our panties
like pale rinds on the sand
and swam out into that black lake, blameless
under those million Michigan stars.
We were so young then,
my body not yet parted by a man,
yours, barely smarting from the fetus
that was sucked from its womb. Think
how it was then, not to feel stones
under foot, our strong arms skimming
the water like loons.

Sezisman

Haitian women have a word for your three lost babies
and two suicide attempts so close in the family,
for the way you think troubles are bound to keep coming,

strung one on another like the shiny drops of shocking pink
the *marchanns* sell in the Iron Market. They demand
ten dollars from a *blan,* but will take fifty cents

for a string of the seeds they call Job's tears
after the one who refused to curse God and die
while he scraped his own boils with pot shards.

These women could spend their whole lives in black,
when the only new clothes get sewn for mourning
their mothers, their lovers, their sons.

If they take to their beds, these women think back
to the last bad news that left them stunned,
squatting over wash stones in the sun.

Sezisman, they say, can make you sick even months later,
but, Ellen, they say if you cry when you hear the news,
it may not take your life.

This Year's Seder

for Ellen

As your husband tips his wineglass
for each plague on ancient Egypt,
do those red drops on the china
remind you? Do you count each plague
as your plague? Count the bitter herb
and egg as your pain and the embryos
lost without graves? The matzoh
is your belly that never rose, the salt,
your tears and the comfort you found alone.

This year, your body is a strong house,
and in this candlelight
wine is the blood you place
on the lintel and doorpost
each time you bring the cup to your lips.
The Destroyer, a hot wind from the desert,
passes over the secret leavening
you bring to this feast,
the child singing with you
in your womb.

Mother

I do not write to you
that a boy, knifed in the groin,
fell behind the band shell
where I ushered for Shakespeare-in-the-Park.
I warned people to stay seated,
to ignore sirens and lights
throbbing red in the humid night.
Now I can't sleep, and it's too hot
to close windows. Down below, men curse
in the street, breaking bottles,
and tomorrow I'll find stains on the walk.
I spare you these details
as sweetly as you spared me
all those years of lawn and cricket song,
all those August days you scalded skins
off tomatoes and squeezed those hot globes
into hundreds of jars. You picked corn
until your arms welted red, then cut off
the kernels, your wrists sticky with its milk—
all those identical days of your life,
culminating in the sparkling arch
of the sprinkler hose,
caught in porch light.

For Weatherly, Still in New York

1984

Pennsylvania's so swelled with July it's shocking.
Leaves fatten on afternoon sun, and oatfields
stir like water in the wind. Leave Second Street.
Your black cat ran screaming onto the stoop,
and the neighbors think you kick it around.
You just might. Here fireflies rise
off the cornfields, and apricot clouds
butt against the mountain's spine. The sun
sets so violently it hurts something inside.
You can't get that kind of violence in New York.
You tried to stab a cop in McSorley's last week,
you were that drunk. This place could make you well.
Night, a black healer, comes so dark it kills
as it cures. Stars slice your fingers
if you try to catch them, falling.
This is no dinner invitation: nights last winter
I fussed over cold muffins or a skin on the stew,
and you came late or not at all. Weatherly,
you can't stay on the Lower East Side,
or at least stay there and stay sane.
Come, lose your lease for this place.

Piano, New York

Anywhere, like Idaho, women like our aunts
would save quarters in cups or sell pies
to buy one like this. They'd put it in a parlor
for hymns and rub it with lemon oil each week,
but here an old piano comes with the apartment,
and no one will pay movers to hoist
the beast out the window on ropes.
We think we've no choice but to saw into its side
that shines like the side of a horse.
We save the real ivory keys in shopping bags
and yank out the rack of purple felt mallets.
Behind it all is a harp, tall as the whole piano
and sprayed with gold. When wing nuts are loosened,
the strings twang then hang slack. We stop
for a moment, then rasp through its frame
with hacksaws and drag the thing, piece by piece,
down three flights of stairs to the street
where people walking by recognize—
just from its insides—a piano.

At the Acme Bar and Grill

In dim light Manhattanites sip margaritas
and suck their fingertips. Who else is wondering
where Buffalo chicken wings come from?
I can't be alone in my memory of calico
bonnets to keep the gray air and stench
of chicken off your hair, or the heavy cart
pushed down dim aisles of hens
cramped into slots like tenements.
How they squawk and peck when you reach
for the eggs that drop without cracking
into wire troughs because of oyster shells
slipped in their feed. The eggs stack
on cardboard flats, a dozen square
and higher than your head. If one drops
you kick it in the gutter, where rats run
at night. Some eggs come smeared with shit
or blood, some huge with double yolks, and once
or twice a week you find one tiny as a robin's.
These I named lucky eggs—rare as luck,
small as luck—I sucked their insides
and saved shells. Who at the bar will admit
he knows how hot a henhouse becomes
under a corrugated tin roof like the restaurant's
ceiling? Or how you blink in the sunlight,
when you finally emerge, your shoes ancient
with dust, your clothes reeking, your ears
full of the dull din of thousands of chickens,
distant as the noise outside a nightclub.

Sunday Night Supper for a Mennonite, 1991

Open a can of great northern beans and think
of a grandmother's hands, thick and speckled
without a band, sorting stones from dried beans
in a dishpan. See her rosebud bib apron
and the wisps of hair escaped from her covering.
Scorch some butter, add some milk, and remember
a gallon mason jar, the inch of thick cream
at the neck. See her shake it before you can drink.
Drain the beans, dump them into the pan. Think how they
pucker their skins, soaking all Saturday afternoon
for a meal that gets eaten in haste before
Sunday night church. Drop bits of bread
into the milk, watch them swell and go limp. Smell
wind off the cornfields blowing in over pews
while she stirs the heat with a cardboard fan,
The Good Shepherd on one side, a seed company ad
on the back. Search the cupboards for a bowl
that's shallow and wide as a dinner plate,
cracked or floral. Hear her shrill voice
above all the rest, "Tis So Sweet to Trust in Jesus."
(She'd been half deaf since she tried to climb the silo
and fell, her bonnet a bloody helmet.) Note
the absence of Lebanon bologna and longhorn,
fill your bowl again. But always eat bean soup alone
or with your own family. Even your lover will find it
bland and not believe ethnics can eat so plain.

The Path to a Man's Heart

Alone in bed, I stroke the empty dish
of skin that sags between my pelvis bones,
knowing now what widows know: next to night
the meals are worse. I eat with cookbooks
propped beside my plate; curries always take me
to the night before I left. How I cooked,
garlic hissing in the wok. How we ate!

A whole week before I left, we did not mention sex,
as though silence could ease our bodies
to the sleep of abstinence, but still
we had to eat. "The path to a man's heart
is through his stomach," my father used to say.
And so, my love, I cooked to fatten us against
these meager months, to burn the craving
from our tongues.

Handling Tools

for Patrick

You take tools from your tackle box
saying needle nose pliers
move paper cuttings too small to touch
but also snip wire. The Exacto knife shapes
fingers without blunting a knuckle
and parts the tails of birds.
The awl pricks dots of glue
like wet braille on paper.
You hold the long scissors
like holding the beak
of the longest-beaked bird
you ever loved. Their crossing slides
like a drop of water between the blades,
gliding back as they open.
You love to force them together
until the drop slides off the tip.
You hold them in that tender web
between finger and thumb
that is white as the underside of a wing,
and cutting, your thumb presses
gently as a gill, against your palm.
When you weave your wrist,
the scissors part paper like water;
the cool dorsal blade
glides like a fin without snagging
fiber, and scales off scraps
with hardly a wrinkle, a ripple.

The View

for Dale

You say you've moved to a place with a view,
and that has changed everything: now you
won't be back to your rooms on the third floor
where we watched the moon rise over the neighbor's
slate roof, and shamrocks in coffee tins
strained for afternoon sun in your kitchen.
There are windows on east and south, you say.
The lake is the color of sky some days;
one blue sinks the whole way down from heaven
to the dirty sands of Lake Michigan.
At night there's no telling ships from stars
in that deep black. Last week, a wind charged
off the lake so cold pigeons froze to the walks,
four iridescent necks just on your block.
But all the cold carcasses in Chicago
mean nothing next to your view. Although
I never held still for your caresses,
I admit your talk makes me jealous:
the way you speak of the lake like a love
and refuse to hang drapes, the way you scrub
panes until they seem to vanish into
the view. And lake and sky embrace you.

Stevious

Stevious slaps the steering wheel
in time to a tape of African drums
that pound like fists on the bones
between my breasts.
Once before, I felt like this,
at the Labor Day parade when I was six,
the big drum pounded those same bones
when fire trucks and majorettes
from Grapeville came in purple,
and their twirler was a man,
lean and black, the only man
I'd ever seen twirl a baton.
He stopped before me, glistening,
and I clapped and clapped till
my fingers hurt for his silver stick,
his lips like pillows you could kiss,
his arms as dark as our best table,
waxed so smooth they must be cool
to touch; fingers would leave prints.
I wanted to twirl like him,
to have eyes the color of my skin
like Stevious, today; the way sweat
slithers down his neck,
I want to trace it with my tongue,
to say his name out loud:
Stevious Koza, to taste it,
repeating the places he comes from:
Soweto, Lesotho, Mozambique.

Knees

Every spring I split a knee.
Mom said, you'll never be a majorette
with knees like that. Sit still.
I squirmed, picked scabs,
everyday at least, peeled the crust
to see if it was clean and pink
underneath. Or watched it bleed—
slowly, like a bloom opening
then the thick red petal
sliding down my shin until
it was stopped by a finger or tongue.

Now knees seldom bleed.
They just work
under hose or jeans,
and I laugh at men who look.
Knees, just gristle on bone,
and there are scars on these.

Riding Bike with No Hands

I have always longed to,
the way I longed to match Mother's
perfect alto those Sundays
she sang into my ear,
hoping her pitch would stay there.

Harder than staying in tune,
it's been years since I tried to ride
no hands, but under this pure sky
I sing "Christ the Lord is Risen, Today,"
surprised I still know the words.

And my hands drop from the bars
in that quickening
I felt long ago when Daddy let go,
and I coasted off in the lawn,

exquisitely balanced, absolved
from all attachment.

Prospect Park, Holy Week

The mean swan has returned to the pond;
the white ducks are back; the wild ducks are out
in the grass, bobbing between dark tufts of ramp;
the drake's green head is the jewel from a cocktail ring.
The sky is streaked with a pale jet stream,
the stretch mark on a mother's belly, and
the late afternoon sun is a bronze fruit
that glazes the pond with its bronze juice.
The black boys on mountain bikes, who pedal fast
as they can down the hill, have drunk that juice,
and the flushed white men who jog in their college shirts
have drunk that juice, and the cyclist with dreadlocks
and shiny black tights pedals his silent racing bike
like that juice was sweet. And you can smell
sweat in your hair and wet earth on the wind
that stirs dried oak leaves and the sheer chartreuse
of the willow. Through the bare trees,
the old Quaker cemetery gleams in the sun
like a mound of polished fingernails.
The squirrels sit up on their haunches,
and the magnolia's black branches
shock the air with their waxy, white blooms.
The meadow has blossomed into
all the colors of sweatshirts,
and the football is back, soaring high
above all of us, the pit of that fruit.

Morning Glories

for Bertha

Would you approve of my wearing your gloves
to do garden work—the navy wool ones
with leather palms? How well they grasp whatever
is left of my life that you would accept:
the worn handle of this rake, the work
that must get done under a gray sky
in cold wind, the first week of the year.
Look, I've gathered a whole coffee tin
of morning glory seeds, the byzantine pods
exploding with pits dark and sharp
as sparrows' eyes. I don't know what I'll do
with these seeds, except save them.
I pull the brittle vines by their roots,
the neat row that grew into thick ropes
then climbed up six feet of cement,
another six feet of chain link fence,
then smothered the barbed wire on top.
The month of your death, this wall was lush
with leaf-hearts and fluttering maroon
and heavenly blue bells that unfurled
new each day, then withered
into used tissues by dusk. You used to say
you'd never visit until I moved from this city,
but now you feel as close as the flesh. Listen:
a sweet, little Puerto Rican girl is knocking
on her apartment window. How strange I must seem,
raking dead vines off the fence,
scattering seeds and straw on my head,
up my sleeves. She has also seen the blossoms
from above. I wave the glove's leather tracing

of your palm, and she runs from the pane.
It will take all I've got to keep enough space
clear for tomatoes next spring, when this plot
comes up all morning glories.

Notes

p. 6   Sleeping Preacher: During the late nineteenth century, several of these unordained men emerged in Mennonite and Amish communities. There are accounts of people from the audience pulling their eyelids, making sudden noises, and even poking the preachers with a needle in an attempt to rouse them from their trances. They posed a special problem, since their spirit preaching made them unaccountable to the processes of community censure—who could silence the direct voice of God?

p. 15   *"Gott ist die Liebe"*: the English name of this hymn is "For God So Loved Us."

p. 18   *Fleissig Lizzies:* busy or productive Lizzies, what we called the ordinary variety of pink wax begonia.

p. 21   *Freindschaft:* extended family, or clan in Pennsylvania Dutch, the German dialect spoken by the Amish.

p. 23   *Arbeite und hoffe:* work and hope, this phrase is inscribed on the title page of the German edition of *Martyrs Mirror,* translated from the Latin printer's seal of an earlier Dutch edition.

p. 34   *Martyrs Mirror:* The complete though seldom used title of this book—commonly found in the homes of Mennonites, Amish, and Hutterites—is *The Bloody Theatre or Martyrs Mirror of the Defenseless Christians Who Baptized Only Upon Confession of Faith, and Who Suffered and Died for the Testimony of Jesus, Their Saviour, From the Time of Christ to the Year A.D. 1660.*

p. 38   *Geschmuade Bonen:* creamed beans

p. 38   *Kartoffelsuppe:* potato soup

p. 39   *Plautdietsch:* a German dialect spoken by the Mennonites who originated in the Netherlands and migrated to Poland, then to south Russia.

p. 39 *Schlopst du? Mein Liebchen, schlopst du?:* Are you sleeping, my darling, are you sleeping?

p. 45 *Sezisman:* Shock or surprise, according to Haitian tradition, a shock so great it can literally scare you to death, immediately or later.

About the Author

JULIA SPICHER KASDORF was born into the Mennonite and Amish community of Mifflin County, Pennsylvania, in 1962. She was raised in Irwin, Pennsylvania, near Pittsburgh, and attended college at Goshen College in Indiana and New York University, where she received her undergraduate and graduate degrees. Her poems have appeared in *The New Yorker* and many other publications. *Sleeping Preacher* was chosen from more than 900 first-book manuscripts as the winner of the 1991 Agnes Lynch Starrett Poetry Prize, which consists of a $2,000 cash award and publication in the Pitt Poetry Series. Currently she is Manager of Development Communications for New York University, and lives in Brooklyn, New York.

Pitt Poetry Series

Ed Ochester, General Editor